Lizzie's Hidden Message

Julie Ellis
Christen Stewart

Australia • Brazil • Japan • Korea • Mexico • Singapore • Spain • United Kingdom • United States

Lizzie's Hidden Message

Fast Forward
Silver Level 23

Text: Julie Ellis
Illustrations: Christen Stewart
Editor: Cameron Macintosh
Design: Stella Vassiliou
Series design: James Lowe
Production controller: Seona Galbally
Audio recordings: Juliet Hill, Picture Start
Spoken by: Matthew King and Abbe Holmes
Reprint: Jennifer Foo

Text © 2007 Cengage Learning Australia Pty Limited
Illustrations © 2007 Cengage Learning Australia Pty Limited

Copyright Notice
This Work is copyright. No part of this Work may be reproduced, stored in a retrieval system, or transmitted in any form or by any means without prior written permission of the Publisher. Except as permitted under the Copyright Act 1968, for example any fair dealing for the purposes of private study, research, criticism or review, subject to certain limitations. These limitations include: Restricting the copying to a maximum of one chapter or 10% of this book, whichever is greater; Providing an appropriate notice and warning with the copies of the Work disseminated; Taking all reasonable steps to limit access to these copies to people authorised to receive these copies; Ensuring you hold the appropriate Licences issued by the Copyright Agency Limited ("CAL"), supply a remuneration notice to CAL and pay any required fees.

ISBN 978 0 17 012696 0
ISBN 978 0 17 012693 9 (set)

Cengage Learning Australia
Level 7, 80 Dorcas Street
South Melbourne, Victoria Australia 3205
Phone: 1300 790 853

Cengage Learning New Zealand
Unit 4B Rosedale Office Park
331 Rosedale Road, Albany, North Shore NZ 0632
Phone: 0508 635 766

For learning solutions, visit cengage.com.au

Printed in Australia by Ligare Pty Ltd
7 8 9 10 11 12 13 21 20 19 18 17

Evaluated in independent research by staff from the Department of Language, Literacy and Arts Education at the University of Melbourne.

LIZZIE'S Hidden Message

Julie Ellis
Christen Stewart

Contents

Chapter 1	**Gran's Treasure**	4
Chapter 2	**Lizzie's Story**	10
Chapter 3	**The Underground Railway**	16
Chapter 4	**Lizzie's Hidden Message**	22

Chapter 1

Gran's Treasure

Beth's mother was a nurse.
When she worked nights,
Beth would stay at her Gran's.
One night, when Beth was doing
a homework essay at her Gran's,
she asked Gran for help.
"Gran, can you please help me?
I have to describe the life
of an American living before
the Civil War."

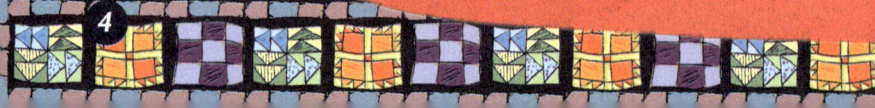

"My most valuable treasure is something from just before the Civil War," said Gran.

"Really? What is it?" asked Beth.

"I'll show you," said Gran. "It's in the chest in the attic."

Lizzie's Hidden Message

Beth watched excitedly as Gran lifted
the lid of the chest.
The treasure might be jewellery,
she thought.
As Gran took out a big square
of material,
Beth peered into the chest.
It was empty.
"Where's the treasure, Gran?"

"This quilt is the treasure," said Gran,
as she carefully unfolded the material.

"What's so special about that?"
Beth asked, disappointed.

"This quilt was made by
my great-grandmother, Lizzie,
when she was 15 years old," said Gran.

"I'm 15," said Beth.

Gran's Treasure

"Yes," said Gran,
"and you have the same name."

Beth looked closely at the quilt.
"Lizzie must have had
a lot of free time,
to make a big quilt like that," she said.

"Lizzie didn't have any free time,"
said Gran.
"She worked hard because
she was a slave."

Beth stared at Gran.
"What do you mean – a slave?"
she asked.

"Lizzie's family was owned by a farmer
in Kentucky," said Gran.
"They had to work for the farmer,
and do what he ordered them to do.
If they didn't work hard enough
they were punished.
They could even be sold."

Beth felt sick.
She was learning about slavery at school,
but she hadn't known her own ancestor had been a slave.
"Tell me about Lizzie," she said.

"It's a long story," replied Gran.
"You've got school in the morning.
I'll tell you next time you visit."

Chapter 2

Lizzie's Story

Beth couldn't wait
to hear more about Lizzie,
so she went to stay the weekend
at Gran's.

On Friday night after dinner,
Gran began to tell Beth about Lizzie.

"Lizzie was born in 1842," said Gran.
Gran explained that Lizzie
had lived in a cabin
on a farm with her parents
and two brothers.
Lizzie's father and older brother
worked in the fields picking cotton,
and her mother and younger brother
worked in the vegetable garden.
Lizzie worked in the farmer's house.

Lizzie's Story

The farmer didn't like Lizzie's older
brother and gave him
the hardest jobs.
Lizzie was scared that one day
the farmer would hurt her brother,
or sell him to another farmer.

"Why didn't the slaves run away?"
asked Beth.

Lizzie's Hidden Message

"Many slaves tried to run away
to the free states," said Gran.
"But most were captured
by slave catchers or tracking dogs.
However, some slaves found
clever ways to escape."

Gran told Beth about a man
called Henry Brown
who hid inside a box,
and then had the box sent
from the slave state of Virginia
to the free state of Philadelphia.

Lizzie's Story

Lizzie was clever, too, Gran explained.
She helped her older brother
and other slaves escape.

Beth was curious.
"How could a 15-year-old slave girl
help adults escape?" she asked.

Lizzie's Hidden Message

"Lizzie was a seamstress," said Gran.
"Every day she went to
the farmer's house,
where she made beautiful clothes
for the farmer's daughters.
She was allowed to keep small pieces
of left-over material,
and she stitched these together
into small patterns.
Then she stitched the small patterns
together to make a quilt.
The patterns all had names such as
'Flying Geese', 'Bear's Paw',
or 'Nine Patch'."

Flying Geese

Bear's Paw

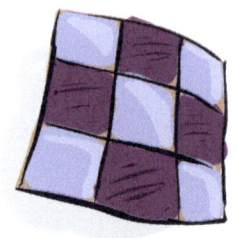

Nine Patch

Lizzie's Story

"But how did she help slaves escape?" asked Beth.

"Lizzie made a quilt!" said Gran.

Chapter 3

The Underground Railway

Gran explained that the quilt was really a map.
Lizzie hung it on the clothes line outside the cabin,
and slaves who were escaping along the Underground Railway would see Lizzie's quilt map and know which way to go.

The Underground Railway

They also knew that Lizzie's cabin was a 'safe house' because a quilt with a sky blue square in the middle meant 'safe house'.

At each safe house, escaping slaves were hidden and given food.

"What was the Underground Railway?" asked Beth.

"Was it a train?"

Lizzie's Hidden Message

"No, it wasn't a real train," said Gran.
"The Underground Railway
was the name given to
the 'safe houses' that led
from the slave states in the south
to the free states in the north.
Escaping slaves would travel
from safe house to safe house.
Lizzie's quilt told them
which way to go
to get to the next safe house."

"Now," said Gran. "I'm tired.
Tomorrow, I'll tell you what each
square means.
You can try to work out the message."

The Underground Railway

"Okay, Gran," Beth said. "Goodnight."
She went off to bed.
Gran had given her a lot to think about.

Lizzie's Hidden Message

The next morning after breakfast,
Gran laid Lizzie's quilt
on the kitchen table.
"The first square
in the top left hand corner
is a Nine Patch, which means fields,"
she explained.

The Underground Railway

"Then there's Pine Tree.
The third square is Bear's Paw,
which means a trail.
Below Bear's Paw is Flying Geese,
which means water.
The square in the bottom right
is called Road To Ohio.
Then we see North Star, Maple Leaf
and Log Cabin.
Now you work out
the hidden message
while I clear away these dishes."

Chapter 4

Lizzie's Hidden Message

Beth stared at Lizzie's quilt.
She imagined she was
an escaping slave,
and tried saying each pattern
out loud.
"Fields, trail, pine tree, water."

The message was too hard to read.
When Gran came back,
Beth asked for help.

Lizzie's Hidden Message

Gran pointed to each pattern.
"The first three patterns mean,
walk past the fields
until you come to the pine tree,
then follow the trail to the water."

"Oh, I get it," said Beth.
"Next, you follow the water
until you come to the road to Ohio.
Then follow the North Star
until you come to the maple trees.
The next cabin you come to
is a safe house."

Lizzie's Hidden Message

"Well done, Beth," said Gran.
"You read Lizzie's message."

"Gran, how do you know about
Lizzie?" asked Beth.

"Because it's a family story," said Gran.
"My gran told me, and one day
you'll tell it to your grandchild.
But right now you have
an essay to write,
and I want you to get an A+."

"I'll try, Gran," said Beth.
"Thanks for sharing Lizzie's story
with me."